In My P

Gay Su Pinnell
Jan Swartz
Colleen Griffiths
Adria Klein

Illustrated by Randol Eagles

Dominie Press, Inc.

The development of the *Carousel Readers* was supported by the Reading Recovery project at California State University, San Bernardino. All authors' royalties from the sale of the *Carousel Readers* will be used to support various Reading Recovery projects.

Publisher: Raymond Yuen
Illustrator: Randol Eagles
Cover Designer: Pamela Pettigrew-Norquist

Published by

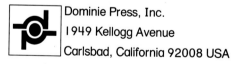

Dominie Press, Inc.
1949 Kellogg Avenue
Carlsbad, California 92008 USA

ISBN 1-56270-199-1
Printed in Singapore by PH Productions Pte Ltd.

7 IT 99

On the way to school,
I found a shiny penny.
I picked it up
and put it in my pocket.   3

Then, I found a round rock.
I picked it up
and put it in my pocket.

4

Then, I found a little blue ball.
I picked it up
and put it in my pocket.

Then, I found a yellow pencil.
I picked it up
and put it in my pocket.

Then, I found a big button.
I picked it up
and put it in my pocket.

Then, I found a dead bug.
I picked it up
and put it in my pocket.

When I got to school,
my teacher asked,
"What do you have
in your pocket?"

9

"I have a shiny penny," I said.
"That's nice," said my teacher.

"I have a round rock," I said.
"That's nice," said my teacher.

"I have a little blue ball," I said.
"That's nice," said my teacher.

"I have a yellow pencil," I said.
"That's nice," said my teacher.

"I have a big button," I said.
"That's nice," said my teacher.

"I have a dead bug," I said.
"Oh, no!" said my teacher.
"Put it here."

15

"Now we all can see it."